In My Refrigerator Box

Elizabeth Fierro
Illustrations by Désirée Fierro-Wohlfarth

iUniverse books may be ordered through booksellers or by contacting:

iUniverse
1663 Liberty Drive
Bloomington, IN 47403
www.iuniverse.com
844-349-9409

Because of the dynamic nature of the Internet, any web addresses or links contained in this book may have changed since publication and may no longer be valid. The views expressed in this work are solely those of the author and do not necessarily reflect the views of the publisher, and the publisher hereby disclaims any responsibility for them.

Any people depicted in stock imagery provided by Getty Images are models, and such images are being used for illustrative purposes only.
Certain stock imagery © Getty Images.

ISBN: 978-1-6632-1540-6 (sc)
ISBN: 978-1-6632-1541-3 (e)

Library of Congress Control Number: 2020925815

Print information available on the last page.

iUniverse rev. date: 12/31/2020

In My Refrigerator Box

I sewed a dress made
out of flames

And built a castle
from some rocks

Went
back
in
time

and saved
the
world...

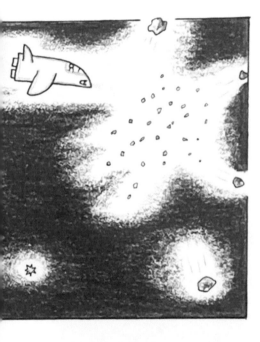

In my refrigerator box

I bought some crayons

and drew a palace

Then fought a
dragon 'til it died

Set fire to the villain's tower

And cheered the princess
when she cried.

In my dark brown
cardboard prism, I changed
the colors of the sky

Now purple clouds
hang from above
And catch us when we fly.

I climbed the highest mountain

And found a cure for chickenpox

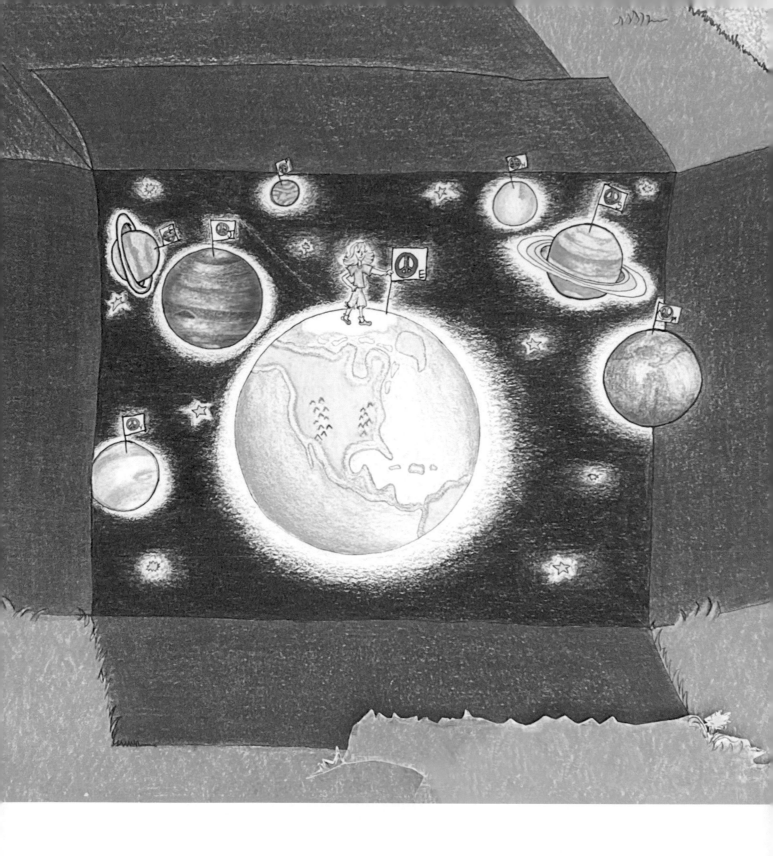

Conquered the world and
all the planets...
In my refrigerator box.

Printed in the United States
By Bookmasters